"EVERY INDIVIDUAL
MATTERS. EVERY
INDIVIDUAL HAS A
ROLE TO PLAY. EVERY
INDIVIDUAL MAKES A
DIFFERENCE."

—JANE GOODALL

PEACE LOVE ACTION!

EVERYDAY ACTS OF GOODNESS

FROM A TO Z

TANYA ZABINSKI

FOREWORD BY ANI DiFRANCO

PLUM BLOSSOM
BOOKS

BERKELEY, CALIFORNIA

CONTENTS

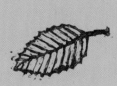

FOREWORD
ANI DIFRANCO

IN THIS BOOK, you will encounter many stories of extraordinary people. Some may be familiar and others may be new to you. To this inspiring collection I would like to add one more story: of the author herself, my friend Tanya.

Tanya and I have been traveling on parallel paths for thirty years now. When we first met in a painting class at Buffalo State College, I was all of eighteen, and she was twenty-five. We decided to become housemates and moved in with another budding artist, Laylah Ali. Our mailbox, with its trifecta of ethnic names, read like a microcosm of Buffalo itself. I don't know if there was something special in the water in that little apartment, but each of us went on to create independent and self-directed careers making socially conscious art.

Tanya's positive, simple art works have manifested in the world in a myriad of ways, from the prints and paintings that hang all over my house, to the murals that brighten various public spaces in our hometown, to the hand-printed shirts that walk the globe transmitting her inspired imagery. She, like any artist, has had to be very creative not just in the making of her art, but also in devising ways to turn that art into a livelihood. What is most extraordinary is the degree of attention and intention she applies to that process. She triangulates her creativity with a high degree of social responsibility, and all of her choices flow from there. From her example, I have learned a lot about how to live within a model of sustainability and care.

Tanya studies herbalism and homeopathy and attended to me around the birth of both my children. She was recycling and actively participating in food cooperatives long before I or the culture at large seemed to understand the implications of such things. She prints her textiles with nontoxic, water-based inks. When she and her husband saw that Buffalo lacked a truly community-based arts festival, they founded the Elmwood Avenue Festival of the Arts, which now brings together thousands of people every August.

I could go on about the many wonderful forms that Tanya's art and activism have taken, but I think as you turn the pages of this book you will get a sense of the woman behind it. The artwork herein and the stories that accompany them teach and inspire. They warm the body with feelings of hope and invigoration. They challenge the mind to view the world in a positive and life-affirming way. These are the gifts Tanya gives me as a friend and comrade. I'm excited that this book will bring her wisdom and worldview, her joy and generosity to ever more people. Within these pages, you can meet my friend and a host of other peaceful activists, and I hope you will find yourself as inspired as I do.

Ani DiFranco
January 2019

INTRODUCTION
WHAT IS A PEACEFUL ACTIVIST?

DR. MARTIN LUTHER KING JR. SAID, "Peace is not merely a distant goal we seek, but a means by which we arrive at that goal." He practiced this as he led a movement for racial equality that continues to this day. Peaceful activism is not only what we do; it's also how we do it.

My most basic definition of a peaceful activist is someone who works to choose love over fear, just as Dr. King did. We can direct love toward ourselves, toward our family and friends, and toward many people and situations. Being a peaceful activist doesn't mean we need to love the actions of an oppressor, but if we strive to see points of light within even the most harmful person or circumstance, it can help us act out of love and not fear.

Gandhi told us, "If we could change ourselves, the tendencies in the world would also change. As a man changes his own nature, so does  the attitude of the world change toward him." Being a peaceful activist is not about blaming someone else—or ourselves. It's about doing what we have the power to do. It involves inner work and outer work. It's personal and communal. In the image to the left, the flower represents beauty, inspiration, and inward action. The hammer signifies strength and outward action. A peaceful activist needs both inspiration and action.

As a child, I thought that to be a helpful force in the world, I'd need to wait until I was older. I imagined joining the Peace Corps and helping people in far-off lands. But what if we see peace not as something we need to wait to practice until we're older? What if we can practice it right now? Even as an adult, I often feel like my capacity for personal action is in short supply when just keeping up with the daily grind can be more than enough to manage. Can we see peace not as something we attend to after our daily grind, but something we do right in the middle of it? What if we can give attention to what's going on inwardly and work to develop peace of mind, so that, like a smile, it naturally spills outward?

Peace is a universal cause, but the way each person advances that cause is highly personal. In this book I share a variety of ways individual people have found to open to love and advance peace. In compiling these stories of peaceful activists, I discovered many commonalities. The main trait that all the activists share is that they each have love as a motivating force. Thich Nhat Hanh says, "True love has the power to heal and transform the situation around us." Even as a child, Jane Goodall expressed a love of animals and nature. Autumn Peltier is still a child, and she advocates for clean water from a heartfelt connection to it.

Hand in hand with love is perseverance; all the activists faced obstacles that required them to stay strong and carry on. As Rachel Carson wrote her groundbreaking book *Silent Spring*, she was beset by serious illnesses. Although this slowed her writing down, her deep love of nature and her desire to protect it gave her the will to persevere. All of the peaceful activists also share an unconventional spirit. They used creative thinking. They thought and acted outside the box. They questioned the status quo. Shirley Chisholm defied convention by speaking up when most would have remained silent. She also blazed a trail by being the first African American woman in the United States Congress. At a time when most music schools believed talent was inherited and required students to show musical aptitude before accepting them, Shinichi Suzuki opened his music school to anyone, including three-year-old children. Instead of running away from discrimination, Valarie Kaur moves toward it to document it, hold it to the light of day, find what needs healing, and let in love.

Several of the peaceful activists tied together two interests or issues in a unique way. Thich Nhat Hanh integrates spirituality with practicality. Pete Seeger fused music with social and environmental activism. Wangari Maathai combined environmental issues with social issues. Jon Kabat-Zinn applies modern science to ancient practices of yoga and meditation. Ruth Johnson Colvin integrates building self-esteem into her adult literacy program. Leah Penniman connects farming with racial justice, community building, song, dance, health and healing, and even prayers and celebration.

Andrew Bienkowski and Azim Khamisa both illustrate the ability to spin hardship into gold. Banished to a prison camp in Siberia, Bienkowski was still able to find something for which he could be grateful. When his only son was murdered by a gang member, Khamisa was able to transform his pain into compassionate action. Both men chose love over anger, and in healing their own wounds, they became a light for others. No one of these heroes stood alone. The activists all had support—guides, mentors, or helpers. Whether from a parent, a partner, a friend, a teacher, an organization, a spiritual practice—or, in Norman Cousins's case, some Marx Brothers films—each person received a form of assistance. All of these activists used the skills they had and developed new skills as needed. They stretched themselves. They grew—and, in the process, they illuminated the way for many.

The Japanese poet Ikkyū wrote: *Many paths lead from the foot of the mountain, but at the peak we all gaze at the single bright moon*. Learning about the paths of these peaceful activists has shone a light on my own path. It's helped me find places where I can open to love. It is my wish that these stories, and the art that goes with them, add light and beauty to your path, as we all make our way up the mountain.

AUTUMN PELTIER (2003–)

A IS FOR APPRECIATE

PUBLIC NOTICE: DO NOT DRINK THE WATER

This sign is one of many posted near Autumn Peltier's home. It refers to the tap water. Its message has made her worry, cry, get mad, and speak out as a water advocate.

Autumn Peltier is Anishinaabe from Wikwemikong First Nation Unceded Territory on Manitoulin Island in the Great Lakes. She lives surrounded by water. In the Indigenous worldview, water is sacred; it is alive and has a spirit. Water needs to be treated with dignity and respect.

It might seem natural then, that the issue of water is important to Autumn. Embedded in her First Nations culture is a code of respect for all living things. Autumn's mother has taught her the Seven Grandfather Teachings and the importance of water since Autumn was a toddler. Autumn's great-aunt, Josephine Mandamin, was a respected

appreciate

elder and water-walker. She walked more than 250,000 kilometers, around all five Great Lakes, to draw attention to and create awareness of the importance of water.

With the wisdom of her culture and with inspiration and mentorship from her mother and great-aunt, Autumn is a water warrior. Starting at a community meeting when she was only eight years old, Autumn has taken up this role with clarity, strength, and poise. Wearing traditional clothing, incorporating traditional language and song, and weaving the ancient wisdom of her people into her speeches, Autumn has spoken up on behalf of the water.

"Water is the lifeblood of Mother Earth."

Autumn has carried her message far and wide. In 2015, she and a fellow youth water advocate represented Canada at the Children's Climate Conference in Sweden. Following that, Autumn expressed her concern to Justin Trudeau, the Prime Minister of Canada, over the expansion of the Trans Mountain Pipeline. She has been nominated twice for the Children's International Peace Prize, for her advocacy of worldwide clean drinking water. And on World Water Day in 2018, at only thirteen years old, she spoke to the United Nations General Assembly in New York. Standing on a stool to reach the microphone, Autumn Peltier told the General Assembly to "warrior up" when it comes to protecting clean drinking water for future generations.

As Autumn Peltier says, "Mother Earth has been in existence for billions of years. She doesn't need us, but we need her."

WHAT YOU CAN DO

☐ What are some things in nature that are easy to take for granted, but if you didn't have them, they'd be hard to live without?

☐ How does appreciation grow? What are some ways to show appreciation? What can you do today to show appreciation?

☐ As water travels from the sky to the land to the ocean, it moves in basins called "watersheds." Find out what your local watershed is. Find out the source of your drinking water. Find out where your sewer water goes.

☐ Visit a water treatment plant and/or a sewage treatment plant.

☐ Participate in a clean-up project at your nearby waterway.

☐ Count how many times in one day you come into contact with water.

☐ Celebrate World Water Day on March 22.

☐ Celebrate Indigenous Peoples' Day on the second Monday in October. Learn about the reasons people in the United States have replaced Columbus Day with Indigenous Peoples' Day.

☐ The Seven Grandfather Teachings are a part of Native American culture that provides ethical stepping stones. Learn more about them!

DID YOU KNOW?

There is the same amount of water on Earth now as there was when Earth was formed.

Nearly 97 percent of the world's water is salty or otherwise undrinkable.

THICH NHAT HANH (1926–)

B IS FOR **BREATHE**

THICH NHAT HANH (pronounced *tik n'yat hawn)* was born in Vietnam. When he was sixteen, he became a Buddhist monk, making a promise to become peaceful, happy, and calm, and to be kind and loving toward all living beings.

He learned how to meditate and concentrate. As he grew older, he discovered a way to breathe so he could stay calm and loving even in very difficult situations. When we are aware of our breathing, we get in touch with ourselves and how we are feeling. Try it! Feel the sensation of the air coming in and out of your nose. Put your hand on your belly. Feel how it rises and expands as you breathe in, and falls as you breathe out. Breathing calmly and mindfully, we become fully present, fully alive.

When Thich Nhat Hanh was twenty years old, there was a war in Vietnam. He and his friends had a choice: remain in their monasteries

breathe

practicing meditation, or help people suffering from the devastation of the war. Thich Nhat Hanh chose to do both.

He and his friends trained thousands of young students in practical skills like farming, building, and medicine, so they could go out and help rebuild villages destroyed by the bombs. He taught the students how mindful breathing could help them stay brave and compassionate in dangerous situations.

Thich Nhat Hanh also took part in international peace talks to end the war. He established peaceful communities where people of all ages can go to learn the art of mindful living. He realized there are wars, not only because humans have a lot of bombs and

"Smile, breathe and go slowly."

weapons, but because we have a lot of fear, anger, and hatred. But if we know how to breathe gently, and release stress and tension in our body, we can practice compassion toward our feelings of fear, anger, and hatred, and we can meet them with kindness. We can also practice compassion toward others. In this way, we learn to live in peace.

Thich Nhat Hanh has written more than a hundred books on meditation, mindfulness, and peace! He's also trained many young monks and nuns to continue teaching mindfulness, so that more people can learn how to practice peace and how to create a world without war.

WHAT YOU CAN DO

☐ When you breathe in and breathe out, can you feel your breath moving through your body, from your nose down your throat, into your chest, and then into your lungs? Can you feel how your breath affects your whole body—your shoulders, your stomach, and even your hands and feet?

☐ Let yourself feel peaceful and relaxed as you breathe naturally. Just by breathing mindfully, you are building peace.

☐ In difficult moments, pay attention to how your breathing changes. Do you ever hold your breath? Enjoy letting it go.

☐ Next time you feel nervous or anxious, whether it's taking a test, giving an oral report, being up at bat, performing or anything else, pay attention to your breath. Is it shallow? As you allow it to deepen, observe if you feel calmer.

DID YOU KNOW? All living beings breathe. No matter what our beliefs or our politics are, we all have an in-breath and an out-breath that we can be aware of. And we can let this awareness nourish us throughout the day.

JOHN MUIR (1838–1914)

C IS FOR CONSERVE

JOHN MUIR was a Scottish-born American naturalist, farmer, inventor, sheepherder, explorer, writer, and conservationist. He had a deeply personal and spiritual relationship with nature—he felt cleansed by nature, inspired by nature, in awe of nature. The living world filled him with peace and freshness and energy. He thrived outdoors, in the pure open air. He believed that God is revealed through nature.

John Muir's intense relationship with the natural world created a desire to protect and defend nature from human devastation. He began to do this by writing articles for leading magazines that brought him national attention. His writing was so infused with conviction about the sanctity of nature, he inspired millions of readers, including presidents and members of Congress, to take action to help preserve large national areas.

conserve

"Climb the mountains and get their good tidings."

In 1903, President Theodore Roosevelt accompanied John Muir on a three-day wilderness trip to Yosemite. John was able to convince the president to make Yosemite Valley part of a larger Yosemite National Park. While some people pressed for the controlled, profitable use of forests, John was deeply opposed to the commercialization of nature. He referred to the national parks as "places for rest, inspiration, and prayers."

Working with the Sierra Club, which he helped found in 1892, John was involved in the creation of national parks such as Sequoia, Mount Rainier, Petrified Forest, Yosemite, and the Grand Canyon. He is often called the father of our national park system. And the Sierra Club is now the country's largest and most influential environmental organization.

John Muir said, "Nature's peace will flow into you as sunshine flows into trees. The winds will blow their own freshness into you, and the storms their energy, while cares will drop off like autumn leaves."

WHAT YOU CAN DO

☐ Do you feel conservation of the natural world is important? Why? Can you think of some of the ways we can conserve? Below are a few more ways to add to your list. Remember, when we conserve in any way, we help the natural world.

☐ Visit a national park. If possible, volunteer at one.

☐ Volunteer with a Sierra Club chapter, land conservancy, or Waterkeeper alliance near you.

☐ Pack your lunch in reusable containers, and use a reusable lunch bag.

☐ Walk, bike, and use public transportation.

☐ Organize or help with a neighborhood or waterway cleanup.

☐ Compost food scraps and try not to waste food.

☐ Reduce, reuse, recycle!

DID YOU KNOW? There are fifty-eight national parks and 765 national wilderness areas in the United States. Canada has forty-seven national parks and preserves and fifty-four national wildlife areas.

MARTIN LUTHER KING JR. (1929–1968)

D IS FOR DREAM

MARTIN LUTHER KING JR. grew up in the United States in a time when the law treated people differently depending on the color of their skin. If their skin was dark, like his, they had to drink from separate water fountains, ride in the back of buses, and go to separate schools, hotels, and restaurants. Segregating people according to their skin color is due to racism, the false belief that light-skinned people are superior to darker people. Racism had been used to justify slavery in the United States for 246 years. Even though slavery had been outlawed in the United States since 1865, there were still remnants of racism written into the laws. Martin wanted to change that. He dreamed of people of lighter and darker skin all being fairly and equally treated. He imagined a day "when people will not be judged by the color of their skin, but by the content of their character."

dream

In his famous "I Have a Dream" speech in 1963, Martin imagined "the sons of former slaves and the sons of former slave owners will be able to sit together at the table of brotherhood."* With this dream, Martin led the United States toward racial equality.

Many people were rightfully angry at the unjust way black Americans were being treated, and they wanted to fight back with violence. Martin himself had been threatened, assaulted, arrested, and imprisoned. But Martin knew that to achieve his dream of former adversaries sitting together at a table of friendship, the table needed to be set with respect and peace, forgiveness, and acceptance.

He also understood that in the process of gaining their rightful place of justice, he and fellow civil rights activists "must not be guilty of wrongful deeds." He urged them, "We must forever conduct our struggle on the high plane of dignity and discipline. We must not allow our creative protest to degenerate into physical violence."

Martin was a Baptist minister and was influenced by the teachings of Jesus and Mahatma Gandhi. After visiting Gandhi's birthplace of India, Martin said, "I am more convinced than ever before that the method of nonviolent resistance is the most potent weapon available to oppressed people in their struggle for justice and human dignity."

Martin Luther King Jr. saw that violence leads to a cycle of anger, fear, revenge, and division. Nonviolence and civil disobedience, in contrast, he saw, appealed to people's consciences and allowed for reconciliation and unity. By imagining the ideal outcome, and by holding a vision of unity, he helped the United States adopt civil rights laws that gave equal rights to African Americans.

---

* It is more true to life to say "person who enslaved others" instead of "slave owner" as no one can rightfully own another person, but this is how people spoke in Dr. King's time. As the way we see things changes, language changes too.

WHAT YOU CAN DO

☐ Envision what peace would look like in yourself, your family, your school, your town, your country and your world. What would peace look like between different sexes, genders, races, religions, political parties, and countries? Do different people share the same dreams?

☐ Think about where dreams begin. How do they become reality?

☐ Watch Dr. King's "I Have a Dream" speech.

☐ Write your own "I Have a Dream" speech.

☐ Create a banner on which you and your friends can write your dreams for a peaceful world.

☐ Visit the King Center in Atlanta, Georgia, or a peace center near you.

DID YOU KNOW?

Dr. King's ability to get people to share his dream continues to this day. There are more than nine hundred streets and seventy-seven schools in the United States named after him.

The United States passed the Civil Rights Act of 1964, which outlaws discrimination based on race, color, religion, sex, or national origin. It prohibits racial segregation in schools, public accommodations, and employment.

RUTH JOHNSON COLVIN (1916–)

E IS FOR EMPOWER

CHARGED WITH THE JOB of entertaining her four younger siblings on cold winter Chicago Sundays, in an age before computers or even televisions, fourteen-year-old Ruth Johnson invented her own game. With eyes closed, each child would spin the globe and point. Wherever their finger landed, they would research that location in the encyclopedia and write a report about it.

Ruth Johnson Colvin's early interest in education and foreign countries carried through her life. Later, as a wife, mother, and active church member, Ruth persuaded her church to collect donations for a literacy campaign in Zambia. "The perception was," she said, "there was no illiteracy in America." In 1961, when a study revealed that more than eleven thousand adults in her own hometown of Syracuse, New York, could not read or write, Ruth was shocked. "Why doesn't somebody do something?" she wondered.

empower

That somebody turned out to be herself. She began with no teaching degree and no knowledge about teaching adult literacy. Her outlook was, "If you do it with love, it will work out." Ruth trained, researched, and networked. She developed a program to train tutors, who would then teach adults basic reading and writing. Ruth's model used a one-on-one, tutor-learner partnership that allowed for personalized lessons. She simplified and democratized a task that had previously been the realm of the professionally trained.

Starting with the first tutors from Ruth's women's church group in 1962, the program turned into a national organization by 1967, known as Literacy Volunteers of America. In 2002, it became what it is today: a worldwide organization called ProLiteracy. Having grown from a small church group to an international organization in forty years, Ruth's effort clearly met a need. Many people rose to meet that need, and Ruth attributes the success of the program to those volunteers: "We all know it's never one person—it's each of us doing our part."

"If you believe in your idea, you go from there."

Ruth believes that with the right approach, almost anyone can become literate. Sometimes this can mean the difference between life and death. In Haiti, for example, children die because their parents can't read the instructions on medication and water purification systems. When these systems fail, children can die from worms, parasites, and diseases carried in bad water.

Ruth and her husband have crisscrossed the globe to provide training in developing countries, at the invitation of ministries, universities, and governments. In training tutors, Ruth Johnson Colvin models the qualities that she advocates: patience, respect, and enthusiasm. "To me," she says, "one way to get peace is for us to get to know each other. Specifically. One on one."

WHAT YOU CAN DO

☐ The definition of *empower*, is "to make someone stronger and more confident." Does reading empower you? What do you imagine life would be like if you were unable to read?

☐ Do you have a skill, talent, or ability that you feel empowers you? Is there a way for you to share it?

☐ Is there an interest you'd like to pursue that would empower you? Is there a way for you to develop it?

☐ Do you think Ruth Johnson Colvin sacrificed her own needs to empower others?

☐ What do you imagine Ruth Johnson Colvin gained from teaching literacy? What might you gain from teaching those around you?

☐ If you were a teacher, how could you encourage your students?

☐ Tell the teens and adults you know about ProLiteracy.

DID YOU KNOW?

There are estimated to be 781 million illiterate people in the world over the age of fifteen, and two-thirds of them are women.

Illiteracy, especially for adults, can feel humiliating. Recognizing this, Ruth Johnson Colvin built a confidence-booster into her tutoring method. The student first tells the tutor about something at which they excel, and the tutor writes it down and uses it as the first reading lesson. That way, even if reading is hard, the student can still have pride in the subject.

LEAH PENNIMAN (1980–)

F IS FOR FEED

WHEN A BLACK PERSON wants to be a farmer in the United States, sometimes people see that as taking a step backward, into the time of slavery. But Leah Penniman doesn't see it that way. When her grandmother's grandmother's grandmother, Suzie Boyd, was taken into slavery from West Africa, she and others braided seeds into their hair. They didn't know what their future held, but they were hoping it would include land.

Leah Penniman's ancestors had a connection to the land that dated back tens of thousands of years. They had a history of innovating and finding solutions to solve hunger without destroying the planet. Organic, sustainable practices aren't a new invention—Indigenous people all over the world used these practices. And intertwined with growing food to feed themselves, they practiced reverence for the earth and reverence for their community.

feed

Now, Leah Penniman is calling black and brown people back to the land, to reclaim their ancestral connection. What does this reclamation look like? It looks like Soul Fire Farm.

Soul Fire Farm was started in 2006 as a family farm by Leah Penniman and her husband, Jonah Vitale-Wolff, just outside of Albany, New York. It marries ideals of racial justice and food justice with down-to-earth, roll-up-your-sleeves farming solutions. They grow more than eighty kinds of fruits and vegetables, raise meat, and have laying chickens. They deliver their food to people, many of whom would not otherwise have access to good food, including refugees, immigrants, and folks with an incarcerated family member. Approximately eighty families from their community pay on a sliding scale, according to their ability.

"With deep reverence for the land, and with the wisdom of our ancestors, we work to reclaim our collective right to belong to the earth."

Soul Fire Farm does all of this using Afro-Indigenous farming methods that improve the quality of the natural environment. And, not by accident, these practices also improve the quality of the community. Instead of the cold producer-consumer relationship, Soul Fire Farm cultivates relationships with their member families that foster mutual commitment, mutual respect, and shared appreciation.

Beyond its own local community, Soul Fire Farm also reaches out to the broader community. Culturally relevant training programs are offered for Black, Latinx, and Indigenous aspiring farmers. Additionally, Soul Fire Farm offers a model of what the world can look like if we care for the earth, care for the community, and build an organization that reflects our values.

WHAT YOU CAN DO

☐ If you had to leave home and didn't know if you'd ever return, what would you take with you for survival and security?

☐ Leah Penniman has sought out mentors and invited them into her life. At times when she was ready to give up on farming, her mentors gave her the support and encouragement to keep going. Do you have any mentors, or people you admire? Connect with them! Interview them. Ask about their difficulties, and their joys. Ask if they have advice for you. Film them. Write a report. What did you learn? Did anything surprise you?

☐ Have you ever eaten something that you've planted, grown, and harvested? Try it! You can grow sprouts with just seeds, a jar, and water.

☐ Does your school have a cafeteria that offers healthy, nutritious, local food on its menu? If not, consider talking to the people in charge, to see if you can change that.

☐ Does your school have a garden? If not, it may be something that's possible. You'll never know unless you ask!

☐ Contact your elected officials. Tell them you care about the rights of farmers and farmworkers. Ask them what they're doing to support the people who tend the land.

DID YOU KNOW? The African-American scientist George Washington Carver is one of the founders of modern organic agriculture in the United States.

ALICE WATERS (1944-)

G IS FOR GO LOCAL

IF YOU WERE A STUDENT at Martin Luther King Jr. Middle School in Berkeley, California, some of your classes would include organic gardening and food preparation. You would plant seeds, weed, water, and harvest the vegetables that you grew. Then you would prepare those vegetables to make tasty and healthy meals. Your science, math, and English classes would all tie into this experience.

Students at that school have a woman by the name of Alice Waters to thank for this. She started the Edible Schoolyard, as a way to connect kids to the source of their food.

In many places, highly processed soda, chips, and candy bars are easier to come by than apples, carrots, and fruit juice. Alice Waters wants to change that. She supports the use of local, fresh, nutritious, organic, seasonal, sustainably produced ingredients. She advocates passionately for a food economy that is "good, clean, and fair."

go local

Alice's direction in life was shaped by a combination of experiences. She credits "waking up" to her experience studying abroad in Paris, where she lived near a market and learned to cook with fresh local produce. She says, "When you have the best and tastiest ingredients, you can cook very simply and the food will be extraordinary because it tastes like what it is." She also studied at a Montessori school in London. In the Montessori method of education, practical, hands-on, sensory activities are emphasized. At the University of California, Berkeley, Alice became involved with the Free Speech Movement, and anti–Vietnam War efforts, which also shaped her activism.

Alice Waters crafted her life around her interests in quality food, hands-on education, and activism. In addition to the Edible Schoolyard, she established the Chez Panisse Foundation, to support the Schoolyard and encourage similar programs that use food traditions to nurture, teach, and empower young people. Alice is also an author, chef, and proprietor of fine-dining Berkeley restaurant Chez Panisse, and other restaurants that practice the philosophy she advocates.

On top of all that, Alice is vice president of Slow Food International, a nonprofit organization that promotes, celebrates, and advocates for food that is good, clean, and fair for all.

WHAT YOU CAN DO

☐ Find out what fruits, vegetables, and grains grow in your area.

☐ Do you know any farmers? Do you have any farms near you? Visit a farm where you can pick your own fruit.

☐ Join a farm that's a CSA (Community Supported Agriculture). These are farms that sell their fresh food directly to the customer, benefiting both the farmer and the customer. There are benefits for the farmer and benefits for the customer. What do you think they are? Find out more.

☐ Shop at farmers' markets. Find out about urban farms and community gardens near you and visit them.

☐ Do an analysis of one of your meals. Find out how many miles each item traveled to get to your plate, then add them all together. What are the benefits of lowering that number? See if you can do it.

☐ There's more to going local than just food. Supporting local businesses is also important.

DID YOU KNOW? Every dollar spent at a local, independent business helps your community more than spending a dollar at a national chain. It's call the Local Multiplier Effect. A local, independent business spends more of the money it makes with other local businesses. Each $100 spent at local, independent businesses generates $45 of secondary local spending, compared to only $14 if you had spent that $100 with a chain business.

ELLA BAKER (1903–1986)

H IS FOR HELP

Ella Baker was born in 1903 in Norfolk, Virginia. She grew up listening to her grandmother's stories about life under slavery. Though faced with inhumane treatment, her grandmother retained a dignity and resilience. Her grandmother's example nourished young Ella's sense of social justice and served as lifelong inspiration.

Inspiration was needed to face the social landscape of the early 1900s. Even though slavery in the United States had officially ended forty years before Ella Baker was born, black Americans still didn't enjoy the same freedoms and rights as white Americans. Signs were used to show non-white people where they could legally walk, talk, eat, drink, and rest. There were laws preventing interracial marriage. Voting rights for black people were restricted and denied, sometimes by intimidation and violence.

From the time she attended college in Raleigh, North Carolina, Ella Baker stood up to injustice. First, she challenged school policies

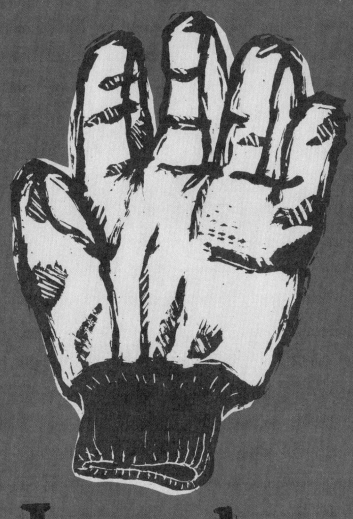

help

that she thought were unfair. Then she joined with many to confront societal and governmental policies that were unjust. She realized that this job required many people to work together, and she played a key role in bringing these people together, with a common goal of racial and economic equality. The movement they started is known as the civil rights movement.

Peaceful protest was a strategy used by many civil rights activists. Their peaceful resistance in the face of harassment, arrest, and violence touched the conscience of the nation and swayed it toward greater equality. One example is a 1960 sit-in that black college students staged at a whites-only Woolworths lunch counter in Greensboro, North Carolina. They politely asked for service, they were denied service, and they refused to leave. Ella wanted to help them and organized a meeting for the student leaders. They formed the Student Nonviolent Coordinating Committee (SNCC), which went on to stage other lunch-counter sit-ins that drew national attention and hundreds of activists—some of whom had to withstand jeers, spitting, and even physical attacks from angry white people. In the end, Woolworths abolished its whites-only policy, and with Ella's guidance the SNCC spawned a new generation of activists.

"We who believe in freedom cannot rest until it comes."

The National Association for the Advancement of Colored People (NAACP) and the Southern Christian Leadership Conference (SCLC) both played large roles in the civil rights movement, and Ella Baker served as a backbone in both of these organizations. She brought people together by guiding, encouraging, and supporting—not dominating. She wanted all the voices to be heard.

Ella Baker continued to be a leader for human rights her whole life.

WHAT YOU CAN DO

- ☐ Ask your grandparents or elders to tell you stories about when they were young, and how it was in the days before cell phones and computers. How has life changed over time?

- ☐ Organize! You can organize a party, a pick-up game, or a performance. You can organize a neighborhood cleanup, a fund-raiser for a cause, or a coat collection for people in need. Take ownership. These actions will help others, and will help you to develop skills of communicating, coordinating, visioning, and sharing.

- ☐ Next time you're a part of a group project, pay attention to how your group functions. Is there a single leader who takes control without paying attention to other voices, or is it more of a roundtable, where everyone's voice is heard? Try using a talking stick or other method to ensure that quiet people have an opportunity to speak.

- ☐ Do you always sit with the same people at lunch? Play a game of mix-it-up with your classmates by having everyone sit with new people.

- ☐ Download the SPLC Civil Rights Activity Book. It is filled with fun projects. (See Resources section.)

DID YOU KNOW? Ella Baker's nickname was "Fundi," which in Swahili means "one who passes skills to the next generation."

EQUAL RIGHTS FOR ALL

SISTER HELEN PREJEAN (1939–)

I IS FOR ILLUMINATE

SISTER HELEN PREJEAN is one of the foremost leaders working to abolish the death penalty, both in the United States and around the world. In thirty-two states in the US, if a person is convicted of murder he or she can be punished with death. After working within the prison system, Sister Helen came to see that the death penalty is unworkable. She observed that it creates more suffering, and she saw that the death penalty system is inevitably flawed, leading to the execution of innocent people.

In 1981, Sister Helen dedicated her life to the poor people of New Orleans and began her prison ministry. She was asked to correspond with a convicted killer, sentenced to die in the electric chair. She agreed, and became his spiritual adviser. Upon his request, she visited repeatedly. During this time, Sister Helen's eyes were opened to the execution process. She wrote the book *Dead Man Walking: An Eyewitness*

illuminate

Account of the Death Penalty. In 1996, the book was made into a major motion picture, which won many awards and increased exposure of the issues with the death penalty.

Sister Helen continues to counsel inmates on death row. She also counsels families of the murder victims, many of whom are filled with anger and hatred. Many feel the best outcome is revenge—they want the criminal to experience the same suffering they caused. But Sister Helen has found that people who follow a course of revenge receive no relief when the criminal is put to death. Instead of achieving closure, families have to witness the death of another person, often after ten or fifteen years of a prolonged and agonizing legal process. The death does not bring back their loved one. Many families of murder victims become strong opponents of the death penalty. They see the path to healing in forgiveness, not in seeking more pain. Forgiveness is not sought for the sake of others but is an act of self-preservation.

"One's commitment has to be renewed every day."

In addition to carrying light into prisons, Sister Helen Prejean carries it into these families' hearts—to help them heal, to keep them alive and open and engaged in life. She sees it as a path, not a single act.

WHAT YOU CAN DO

☐ Saint Martin is the patron saint of beggars and outcasts. Legend has it that as a young man, Martin once cut his cloak in half to share with a beggar who was freezing in a snowstorm. He became known for his ability to bring warmth and comfort to those in need. To honor this spirit of kindness, the holiday of Martinmas was started in France, and is celebrated on November 11 with the making of lanterns. Learn more about Saint Martin and Martinmas, and make a lantern to represent your inner light, and the kindness that you bring to the world.

☐ What do you want to shine your light on? Is there something that you feel needs illuminating?

☐ Do you know of people in need? Share your resources. Donate outgrown clothing. Run a clothing or food drive.

DID YOU KNOW? For each book that you buy from Parallax Press, the publisher of this book, they will send a free book to a person in prison.

VALARIE KAUR (1981–)

J IS FOR JUXTAPOSE

VALARIE KAUR is an American civil rights activist, lawyer, filmmaker, author, and faith leader. She started the Revolutionary Love Project to reclaim love as a force for social justice.

Valarie grew up on farmland in California where her family had lived for one hundred years. But kids at school still saw her brown skin as foreign. They called her a "black dog" and said she would go to hell because she wasn't Christian. At home, her grandfather dried her tears and taught her the words of Guru Nanak, the founder of their Sikh faith: "I see no stranger. I see no enemy." He went on to explain that we all belong to one another. When people hate us, it means there is something inside them that is hurting. We must refuse to hate them back. Instead, we can transform our hurt into something beautiful and good that helps others. Valarie carried this lesson in her heart.

juxtapose

When Valarie was a student in college, a family friend whom she called "Uncle" was murdered in a hate crime. Balbir Singh Sodhi wore a turban as part of his Sikh faith, just like her grandfather. Valarie wanted to hide. But she remembered her grandfather's lesson. She turned her pain into action. She traveled the nation with her camera and made the first-ever film about hate crimes against Sikhs in America. She became a civil rights activist and worked with many different communities across the country, in poor neighborhoods, inside prisons, and at the sites of mass shootings. Whenever she encountered hate and violence, she no longer ran away in tears. Instead, she helped people turn pain into action. Her films, lawsuits, essays, and campaigns helped build movements for social justice anchored in love.

"We will fight not with violence and vitriol, but by challenging the cultures and institutions that promote hate. We will change our opponent through the ethic of love."

Fifteen years after her uncle was murdered, Valarie met the man who killed him. She wanted to hate him, but instead she listened to his story. She no longer saw him as an enemy but as a human being in pain. She forgave him. "Forgiveness is not forgetting," Valarie said. "Forgiveness is freedom from hate." This is the kind of love that Valarie practices— fierce, demanding, and life-giving. Valarie believes that "Revolutionary Love" can be taught, modeled, and practiced. Each day, we can practice loving in three directions—towards others, our opponents, *and* ourselves. When we love ourselves as fiercely as we love others, we lead our lives with joy.

WHAT YOU CAN DO

☐ To *juxtapose* means to position different things side by side that you might not ordinarily see together. What do you think the illustration on page 49 is saying?

☐ Prejudice is a preconceived opinion that is not based on reason or actual experience. See if you can think of an example. How do you think prejudice can end?

DID YOU KNOW? Has anyone ever been prejudiced against you? Instead of denying or forgetting the pain that caused, here's a way that you can try to heal.

Valarie Kaur's Three Steps to Healing after Being Hurt

1. *Hold the hurt.* What does it feel like? Where do you feel it? Is it a lump in your throat? A knot in your stomach? A shortness in your breath? It's important to notice the hurt, because if we push it down it can pop up later.

2. *Let in love.* If you stay in the hurt, it can harden into hate. Instead, imagine a safe and healing place or a person who loves you. Notice how that feels in your body. Do you feel a softening of your shoulders, a warm flush, a relaxed face, a deeper breath?

3. *Choose art and action.* Write a poem or story or letter, paint a picture, start a campaign that makes meaning out of what happened. If you share it, you may discover that you're not alone, and your story may help other people in similar shoes.

COLIN KAEPERNICK (1987–)

K IS FOR KNEEL

COLIN KAEPERNICK is a famous American football player, a political activist, and a vegan. When he was young, he set many high school and college records—in football *and* baseball! The San Francisco 49ers drafted him in 2011, and as the team's quarterback he led them to the Super Bowl less than two years later.

In 2016, Colin began sitting during the National Anthem, to bring attention to police brutality and racial injustice in the United States. He said, "I am not going to stand up to show pride in a flag for a country that oppresses black people and people of color. To me, this is bigger than football and it would be selfish on my part to look the other way."

Then he talked to Army veteran and former Seattle Seahawks player Nate Boyer, and decided that, in order to show respect for those who have served in the US military, he would no longer sit during the anthem. Nate suggested a new form of protest: to kneel. "I expressed

kneel

to him, maybe there's a different way of demonstrating, where you're showing more respect for those who laid down their lives for what that flag and anthem stand for," Nate said of his conversation with Colin. "I suggested kneeling, because people kneel to pray; we'll kneel in front of a fallen brother's grave."

Colin Kaepernick took his suggestion, and started kneeling during the national anthem. Many other players also began kneeling, in solidarity. Many people wanted them to stop, but Colin and the other players kept kneeling at every football game, to remind everyone that freedom, liberty, and justice are meant *for all.*

Colin paid a heavy price for his protest. Despite his abilities, which surpassed many of the new quarterbacks signed in 2018, Colin found himself without a job; team managers around the league decided they didn't want the distraction of his kneeling. Colin had anticipated this possibility, and had been prepared for it.

Colin Kaepernick continues his social action off the field. He has held Know Your Rights youth camps in cities around the country, where attendees learn about their legal rights, financial literacy, and holistic health. Since 2016, Colin has donated a million dollars to organizations working in oppressed communities across the country.

Though Colin Kaepernick no longer plays football for the NFL, he still exerts a strong influence on American society. His silent protest has grown into a social movement that has made powerful institutions like the NFL and the White House ask important questions about patriotism, racial equality, free speech, and protest itself.

WHAT YOU CAN DO

- [ ] The first step in tackling any issue is to raise people's awareness of it. Do you think that Colin Kaepernick's actions have raised awareness around the need to address the problem of racial inequality?

- [ ] Colin Kaepernick intended his act of kneeling to represent respect for the flag, while at the same time calling for our country to be reaching for its ideals of liberty and justice for all of its people. Can you be respectful and critical at the same time?

- [ ] The definition of "patriotic" is "having or expressing devotion to and vigorous support for one's country." Do you think that kneeling during the national anthem is unpatriotic? Is it patriotic?

- [ ] List at least three things that you appreciate about your country.

- [ ] What are at least three improvements that you would like to see made in your country?

DID YOU KNOW?

Colin realized that not everyone is at the same level of understanding or commitment on issues. He was accepting of his fellow teammates, whether they knelt or stood for the anthem. He never tried to push anyone else to do something for which they weren't ready.

Colin has donated to more than forty-one charities, and he has recruited other athletes and artists to match some of his donations, including: Kevin Durant, Stephen Curry, Serena Williams, Usher, Jesse Williams, and more.

NORMAN COUSINS (1915–1990)

L IS FOR LAUGH

NORMAN COUSINS was a political journalist, author of many books, professor, and advocate for world peace. When he found himself paralyzed and in great pain—diagnosed with a condition in which the connective tissue in the spine deteriorates, and given a one in five hundred chance of survival—he felt he couldn't depend on his doctors alone. He knew he had to get involved with his own healing, and he became a kind of detective, working to find out what had brought on his illness.

Norman was able to connect the contraction of his illness to a time of great stress in his life, combined with exposure to toxicity. He had long believed that the biochemistry of human emotions was the key to health, and he was able to put this belief to the test. Observing that negative emotions like fear and frustration had produced negative chemical changes in his body, he went about testing whether positive emotions could produce positive chemistry.

laugh

Norman developed a recovery program, the first step of which was to check himself out of the hospital. With a culture of overmedication, haphazard hygiene practices, and routines that disrupt basic sleep patterns, Norman saw a hospital as "no place for a person who is seriously ill." He stopped taking the prescribed painkillers, codeine, sleeping pills, and thirty-six aspirin a day. Instead he took extremely large doses of vitamin C, along with a positive attitude, love, hope, faith—and laughter.

Norman watched Marx Brothers films and *Candid Camera* episodes to induce laughter. "I made the joyous discovery that ten minutes of genuine belly laughter had an anesthetic effect and gave me at least two hours of pain-free sleep," he reported. "When the pain-killing effect of the laughter wore off, we would switch on the motion picture projector again, and not infrequently, it would lead to another pain-free interval."

"Laughter is inner jogging."

Within a few weeks of starting his recovery program, Norman was back to work. He lived twenty-six years longer than his doctors predicted. We don't need science to tell us that laughter feels good—but Norman Cousins proved that laughter also possesses strong healing powers.

WHAT YOU CAN DO

☐ Consider how laughter can play a part of building peace in the world.

☐ Memorize some funny jokes and share them.

☐ Make up your own jokes and share them.

☐ Practice laughter and happiness daily.

☐ Find a Laughter Club in your area. (See below.)

☐ Start your own Laughter Club.

☐ Celebrate World Laughter Day on the first Sunday in May.

DID YOU KNOW?

As a direct result of reading about Dr. Norman Cousins and the health benefits of laughter that he discovered, in 1995 an Indian medical doctor, Dr. Madan Kataria, developed Laughter Yoga. This led to the formation of Laughter Clubs and even Laughter Yoga University!

Laughter has become an international movement, with a mission of uniting people through the power of laughter.

Laughter brings you into the present moment. Laughter is contagious. Scientists have proven that laughter boosts you physically, emotionally, mentally, and socially.

AZIM KHAMISA (1949–)

M IS FOR
MAKE FRIENDS

CAN YOU IMAGINE making friends with the guardian of your son's murderer? Could you forgive the murderer? Azim Khamisa did both.

In 1995, Azim's twenty-year-old son, Tariq, was delivering pizza in San Diego, California, when he was shot and killed by Tony Hicks, a fourteen-year-old gang member. When Azim received the news of his son's death, friendship and forgiveness were not foremost in his mind. But even in the early stages of mourning, Azim knew he had a choice: he could stay stuck in grief and anger, or he could choose love and forgiveness. He knew that only one choice would honor his son.

With the guidance of a spiritual mentor, Azim transformed his pain into compassionate action. He created a foundation named after his son and dedicated his life to teaching young people the principles of nonviolence and forgiveness.

make friends

Soon after founding the Tariq Khamisa Foundation, Azim contacted the grandfather and legal guardian of his son's shooter, Ples Felix, and they formed a team. A Sufi Muslim whose son was murdered and an African-American Baptist whose grandson was the murderer might appear to be an unlikely team. But neither of them wanted to see other children killed like Tariq, or ending up in prison like Tony. They were both determined to help end the cycle of violence, starting with themselves.

Together, they have been sharing their story in the schools of San Diego since 1996. The foundation has grown to employ ten people working to empower kids, save lives, and teach peace. Their classroom curriculum embodies such themes as empathy, communication, emotion management, and preventing bullying. Their work reaches more than 12,000 students per year.

Five years after the shooting, Azim met his son's murderer, forgave him, and invited him to share in this work for peace upon his release.

"Forgiveness is something you do for yourself."

Before their meeting, Tony Hicks was ready to die in prison. After the meeting, given a purpose to live, he has since completed his GED, and is working on an associate's degree in social work.

Azim is working for his early release, with the belief that "he will be more useful to society working with me and his grandfather than rotting in prison."

Like an alchemist transforming base metal into gold, Azim was able to transform a tragic event into an opportunity for love and unity, by using forgiveness as a central ingredient. Azim says, "Through forgiveness, I've been able to heal."

WHAT YOU CAN DO

☐ Do you wish that people were friendlier toward you? Make an effort to be friendlier to others, and it often comes full circle. Try just smiling at others—you'll be surprised at the effect!

☐ Do you hold grudges? They can weigh you down. Try letting them go. It doesn't mean you have to approve of the other person's past behavior, it just means that you can let that behavior be in the past. Throw that frozen snapshot in the trash!

☐ Invite people to a multi-religion, cross-cultural roundtable.

☐ Food, art, music, and dance are fun ways to share your own culture, or be introduced to the cultures of others. Do a Global Art Project for Peace at your school. (See Resources on page 114)

☐ Start a Peace Club. Your club could focus on increasing inner peace as individuals, between each other, in your wider community, or all three. It could involve anything from organizing a choir, a community garden, or a bicycling group. Tailor it to suit the interests of your club's members.

DID YOU KNOW? Doctors at the Mayo Clinic say, "Letting go of grudges and bitterness can make way for improved health and peace of mind. Forgiveness can lead to healthier relationships, improved mental health, less anxiety and stress, less hostility, lower blood pressure, fewer symptoms of depression, a stronger immune system, improved heart health, and improved self-esteem."

SHINICHI SUZUKI (1898–1998)

N IS FOR NURTURE

SHINICHI SUZUKI'S parents owned a violin factory in Japan. When he was seventeen years old, he started learning to play the violin. At the time, talent was widely thought to be something that some people have and other people don't. But Shinichi observed *who* learns language and how language is learned. He found that just like we can all learn to speak a language, we can all learn to play an instrument, and in much the same way.

So, Shinichi opened a music school that accepted students of all ages and abilities, starting in early childhood and even infancy. He developed a method of music education that mimics the way we learn language. As with language, starting young is helpful, and repetition is important, including practicing and listening. Just as we first learn to speak and then to read words, Suzuki pupils first learn to play music and soon afterward to read notes. Just as we don't need to know how

nurture

to read in order to speak, Suzuki students don't need to read music in order to play. They develop their ear, they develop memorization skills, they develop music reading skills, and these skills can make their music as fluid and natural as language.

Although this method consistently teaches young people to be capable musicians, Shinichi's aim wasn't to produce musical geniuses but to help develop whole, well-rounded human beings. He saw that skills developed by learning an instrument—like discipline and perseverance—are skills that can be carried into the rest of life.

A sense of fun and love and joy were central to Shinichi's life and teaching. Instead of assigning boring exercises, Shinichi used melodic folk songs to teach young students. Shinichi also incorporated rhymes and games, which become increasingly harder as the student advanced. He felt that a key factor for teaching is creating a nurturing environment filled with respect and love.

"Where love is deep, much can be accomplished."

He encouraged parents and teachers to model a high level of character themselves, and to continue to learn and grow.

WHAT YOU CAN DO

☐ Dr. Suzuki had a sign in his school that read, "Character first, then ability." What do you think that means?

☐ Can developing patience and perseverance help you to develop musical ability? If so, how?

☐ What's an interest that you have? How could you nurture it?

☐ Is it easy to practice a musical instrument (or practice sports or any other discipline that requires practice) every day? What's something that could make it easier?

☐ Take something that you know how to do and share it with someone who's interested. It could be teaching someone else how to tie a shoe, or how to skate, ski, read, bake.... Consider: How can you make it more fun?

☐ Do you think your school has enough musical instruments and lessons? You can help by asking that more be provided, if there aren't, and contacting organizations, like Hungry for Music, that provide instruments to schools in need.

DID YOU KNOW? Scientific research has shown that playing an instrument can change the structure of your brain and help it function for the better. It can also improve your long-term memory and lead to a healthier brain. Plus, it's just plain fun!

JANE GOODALL (1934–)

O IS FOR **OBSERVE**

WHEN JANE GOODALL was five years old, her family visited a farm in the countryside. Jane was curious to see how an egg was laid. So she went into the chicken coop and listened and watched and waited for many hours. Her mother, not knowing where she was, became worried. She called the police, and a search party was sent out.

After more than four hours, Jane saw the shape of an egg gradually protrude from between the chicken's legs, and plop onto the straw on the ground. Filled with excitement, she burst out of the chicken coop to tell her mother. Instead of scolding, Jane's mother recognized the sparkle of joy in her daughter's eye and nurtured that.

Jane Goodall applied that same curious spirit, and those same skills of patience and observation, later in life when she conducted a forty-five-year groundbreaking study of the social and family interactions of wild chimpanzees in Tanzania. Before Jane's study, scientists assumed

observe

that only humans used tools and had rational thought, emotions, and personalities. Because Jane was able to observe with an open mind, she was able to dispel her colleagues' false assumptions. Her colleagues were shocked when, in 1960, Jane observed two chimps stripping leaves off twigs to make tools for fishing termites out of termite mounds. Jane also observed that the chimps had unique and individual personalities, used rational thought, and expressed emotions like joy and sorrow.

Jane's family had not been able to afford to send her to college. Many scientists felt skeptical back then that a woman without a degree could upend their field's long-held theories. Jane went on to earn her PhD, which gave her credibility in the eyes of skeptics, but her ability to practice patient observation was developed in childhood: "Like most children before the age of TV and computer games, I loved being outside, playing in the secret places in the garden, learning about nature. My love of living things was encouraged, so that from the very beginning I was able to develop that sense of wonder, of awe...."

"Be patient and don't give up. Be curious and make mistakes."

Jane's sense of compassion extends to animals, people, and the planet. She continues her work today as an animal rights activist, humanitarian, and environmentalist.

WHAT YOU CAN DO

☐ Get involved in Jane Goodall's Roots & Shoots Youth Program to begin mapping your community and discover how best to help your community's natural world thrive. (See Resources on page 116.)

☐ In Jane Goodall's words, "Until we have peace and harmony with the environment, we will never live in a world of peace." Do you agree? How is the environment connected to peace in the world? Do you think it's possible for humans to live in peace with each other and nature?

☐ You don't have to travel to Tanzania to observe living things. They're all around us! Observe the wildlife around you: birds, squirrels, insects, butterflies....

☐ Observe a one-square-foot patch of ground. Record what you see. Dig it up and record what you see underground. Use a magnifying glass.

☐ Feed birds. How many kinds of birds are attracted to your feeder? If you use different food, does it attract different kinds of birds? Learn to identify the birds and their various calls.

☐ Plant a butterfly bush. Plant milkweed. What kinds of butterflies do they attract? What time of day do they come?

☐ Raise butterflies.

DID YOU KNOW? Jane Goodall's discovery in 1960 that chimpanzees make and use tools is considered one of the greatest achievements of twentieth-century scholarship.

WANGARI MAATHAI (1940–2011)

P IS FOR PLANT

WANGARI MAATHAI grew up in rural Kenya. As a child, she would visit a stream near her home to fetch water for her mother. She drank water straight from the stream, and would play among the arrowroot leaves, imagining the frogs' eggs to be strands of beads that she could wear on her neck.

On later visits, she would see thousands of black tadpoles wriggling through the clear water. Wangari describes her childhood land as "abundant with shrubs, creepers, ferns, and trees... Because rain fell regularly and reliably, clean drinking water was everywhere. There were large, well-watered fields of maize, beans, wheat, and vegetables. Hunger was virtually unknown."

Wangari Maathai went to college in the United States and Germany. Upon her return, she found that the fig tree by the stream where she had played with the tadpoles had been cut down, and

plant

the stream had dried up. In fact, many streams had dried up. It became necessary for women to travel long distances to find water, and it wasn't always clean. Much of the land had turned to desert. Commercial plantations had replaced indigenous forests. Tea and coffee plants replaced trees, bushes, and grasses.

As a child, her mother had taught Wangari that the fig tree was sacred. Her cultural traditions forbid it from being cut down. The roots of the fig tree are particularly deep, which enables it to bring deep-running water to the surface. Without these trees, the land dried up.

Knowing what needed to happen to regain fertile land, Wangari organized tree plantings. She saw that employing women to plant the trees offered an added benefit. Employing women offered them empowerment, increasing their autonomy and their social and economic position. Thousands of women planted more than forty-seven million trees in twenty countries in Africa.

Wangari not only planted trees, she planted an idea—which spawned what is called the Green Belt Movement. In her words, "The challenge is to restore the home of the tadpoles and give back to our children a world of beauty and wonder."

WHAT YOU CAN DO

☐ Do you have a favorite tree in your neighborhood? Why is it your favorite? Do you know what kind of tree it is?

☐ Find a knowledgeable person or a book about trees, and learn to identify the trees around you.

☐ Plant a tree! You can use it as an opportunity to commemorate something or someone: a birth, holiday, graduation, or other special occasion.

☐ Grow things! Indoors or outdoors. Sprout sprouts, grow wheatgrass, or plant kitchen scraps: the tops of potatoes or carrots, avocado pits, garlic cloves, onions....

☐ On a sunny summer day, take the air temperature in the full sun, then take the temperature under the shade of a tree. What's the difference? (One tree can do the job of five air conditioners.)

☐ Plant a peace garden, a butterfly garden, or a vegetable garden.

DID YOU KNOW?

A large tree can drink a hundred gallons of water a day! Trees improve water quality by slowing and filtering rainwater and protecting aquifers and watersheds.

Trees lower air temperature by evaporating water in their leaves and they protect the soil from erosion with their roots.

Trees are able to communicate with each other and other life forms through their root systems and network of fungal mycelia. They can defend themselves against attacking insects.

BLACK ELK (1863–1950)

Q IS FOR QUEST

BLACK ELK was a spiritual leader of a Native American tribe called the Oglala Lakota. He was connected to nature, and to what he called the "Great Wakan Tanka," or what many call the Great Mystery. He said that "at the center of the universe dwells Wakan Tanka, and this center is really everywhere, it is within each of us."

To seek guidance, and to connect with the Wakan Tanka within himself, Black Elk went on vision quests. He would go to the woods by himself, with no food, and just watch the birds, the squirrels, even ants and worms. He claimed, "They too are important, and can teach us two-leggeds much if we can make ourselves humble before them." Black Elk made himself humble and listened to their message.

Black Elk was a healer for his people. He said, "Many I cured with the power that came through me. Of course it was not I who cured. It was the power from the outer world, and the visions and ceremonies

quest

"Behold this day. It is yours to make." had only made me like a hole through which the power could come to the two-leggeds. If I thought I was doing it myself, the hole would close up and no power could come through. Then everything I could do would be foolish."

In his book *Black Elk Speaks,* Black Elk shares the story of his life and the ways of his people. At a time when the white man viewed Native Americans as "savages," Black Elk's book revealed the richness and beauty of his people and their deep, spiritual connection to nature.

WHAT YOU CAN DO

☐ To *quest* means to search for something. Black Elk was on a quest for vision, for clarity, and to understand his place in the world. Like him, we can all quest for vision, clarity, and understanding. A quest could be an inward process, or an outward exploration. What might your version of a quest look like?

☐ In some traditions, people are connected to animals that act as spiritual guides, offering inspiration, protection, and wisdom. Is there an animal that holds particular resonance for you? Or does a certain animal often appear in your dreams? Write about the animal. Collect pictures of it. Draw it. Ask it a question. Journal about it. Ask yourself what qualities it has that you admire. Can you develop those qualities in yourself?

☐ Go on a silent walk in which you only listen and observe.

☐ Go camping or canoeing.

☐ Find out more about Indigenous culture by researching who lived on the land where you now live. Do you know where your family comes from?

DID YOU KNOW? There are more than a thousand powwows held every year in North America, which you may be able to attend. Native American culture today is strong!

SHIRLEY CHISHOLM (1924–2005)

R IS FOR REPRESENT

"YOU DON'T MAKE PROGRESS by standing on the sidelines, whimpering and complaining. You make progress by implementing ideas." Those were Shirley Chisholm's words, and that is what she did.

Working as a school teacher in Brooklyn, Shirley observed firsthand how racial and gender inequality affect us from infancy. She wanted to make change from the top, so she went on to become a director for early childhood schools. Seeking more change, from additional angles, Shirley also joined local chapters of organizations like the League of Women Voters and the National Association for the Advancement of Colored People (NAACP).

Noticing that women in politics often assume a background role, Shirley decided to run for office herself. At the age of forty, she became the second African American in the New York State Legislature. Four years after that, Shirley sought—and won—a seat in Congress, becoming the first African-American congresswoman.

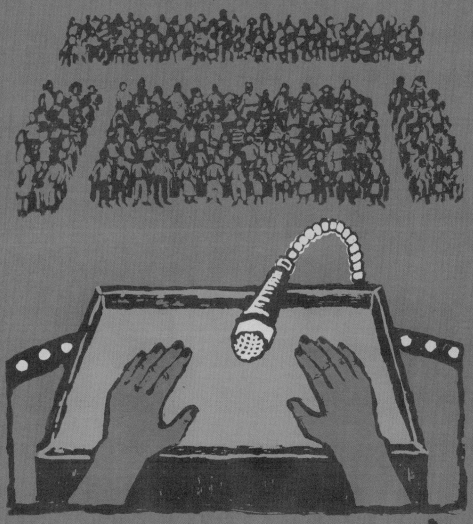

represent

From the very first day she arrived in Washington, DC, in 1968, she stood up. Although Shirley represented an urban district in New York City, the leaders of her party in Congress assigned her to an agricultural committee dealing with rural development and forestry.

"If they don't give you a seat at the table, bring a folding chair."

Typically, newcomers in Congress did what they were told, *especially* on their first day, *especially* if they were black, and *especially* if they were a woman.

But not Shirley Chisholm! She explained to the leadership of her party that there weren't any cotton fields in her district, and that the people who elected her had voted for her hoping that she would represent them, with matters that would help them. Her assignment was changed.

Throughout her thirteen years in Congress, "Fighting Shirley" introduced more than fifty pieces of legislation and championed racial and gender and educational equality, raised awareness about the plight of the poor, and fought to end the Vietnam War.

In 1972, Shirley announced that she would run for president of the United States. She was the first African-American major-party candidate to do so. Although she didn't win the Democratic Party nomination, her passion, her strong principles, and her willingness to stand up for them have paved the way for other underdogs to follow. In Shirley's portrait that hangs on the walls of Congress, her arms are crossed and her stance is bold, as if to say, "I have no intention of just sitting quietly and observing."

WHAT YOU CAN DO

☐ Join a club.

☐ Start a club.

☐ Run for office.

☐ Is there an improvement you'd like to see in your school, community, or family? Find ways to bring it about. Work with others to advance your cause.

☐ Are there other pioneering politicians in whom you are interested? How about pioneers in other fields? Create your own Museum of Pioneering People!

DID YOU KNOW? Since Shirley Chisholm's election to the United States House of Representatives in 1969, forty-six more (and counting) African-American women have been elected to Congress. There is still more work to do to have full representation!

PETE SEEGER (1919–2014)

S IS FOR SING

PETE SEEGER was a singer, songwriter, and folk song aficionado. He used music as a tool for many social and environmental causes, one of which was the Hudson River that flowed near his home. When he saw sewage and dead fish floating on the river, he decided to do something about it.

Combining the fun of music, the joy of sailing, the wonder of the river and the work of cleaning up that river, Pete and his wife, Toshi, started a music and environmental festival called the Great Hudson River Revival. The festival gathers musicians, artists, activists, scientists, educators, and sailors of all ages to share, learn, sail, have fun, and find out how they can contribute to cleaning the Hudson River and to making their own lives more sustainable.

Pete Seeger has received worldwide recognition for his leadership in helping to pass the Clean Water Act. This legislation not only stops

sing

polluters from polluting, it also forces them to clean up their toxic legacy. Parts of the Hudson River that were declared "dead zones" have now been brought back to life.

Whether Pete is singing about a beautiful river, or compost, or justice, or freedom, or love, or molasses candy, he encourages listeners to join in. "I want to leave a song not just in your ear, but on your lips." Pete Seeger's songs travel from the ear to the lips, and also to the heart. His songs and his integrity have inspired generations of people to environmental action and civic responsibility, and to the simple pleasure of singing with friends.

Well I've got a hammer,
and I've got a bell,
and I've got a song to sing all over this land.
It's the hammer of justice,
It's the bell of freedom,
It's the song about the love between my brothers and my sisters,
all over this land.

—Excerpted from the song "If I Had a Hammer"
by Pete Seeger and Lee Hays

WHAT YOU CAN DO

☐ Throughout history, people all over the world have sung while pounding grain, washing clothes, paddling canoes, and during times of sorrow and joy. Pete Seeger used the power of song to bring people together, to educate, to make a hard job more fun, to tell stories, and for pure enjoyment. Does singing have a place in your life?

☐ Next time you drive in the car, instead of turning on the radio, sing a song!

☐ Sing in the shower!

☐ Memorize a song you love.

☐ Write a song about something you did today, something that makes you happy, something that makes you angry, something you want to change, a person or issue that you care about.

☐ You can put your words to a familiar melody, or compose an original melody.

☐ Perform a concert at home or school. Maybe even consider taking it to the street!

☐ Sing at a nursing home or other place where you can bring good cheer.

DID YOU KNOW? When you sing, you change the chemistry in your body, which can relieve anxiety and make you feel happier.

ANDREW BIENKOWSKI (1934–)

T IS FOR **THANK**

ANDREW BIENKOWSKI was five years old when World War II broke out. He and his family and a million others were exiled from their homeland of Poland, to the frozen and inhospitable land of Siberia. They had so little food, Andrew's grandfather chose to starve himself to death in order to allow more food for the younger people. After two years, political conditions shifted, and Andrew and his family were able to leave Siberia.

Even though those two years were so harsh, Andrew was able to look back and say that he was thankful for the life lessons he learned there. If he couldn't find anything for which to be thankful, he felt that all his hard times would have been in vain.

In his book *One Life to Give*, Andrew recounts his experience and shares his lessons. He challenges us to practice what he calls radical gratitude: practicing gratitude not only for wonderful things, but even

thank

for difficult things. Of course no one looks forward to difficult times, he says, but if we recognize value in struggle, we can see the silver lining. Our gratitude softens, heals, and strengthens us.

Andrew also encourages us to be thankful for small things. He learned this from the example of his mother. Even during their hardship, she was still able to find small wonders. Every day she strove to pass that appreciation on to her two young children. A colorful butterfly, a handful of wild strawberries, and the beauty of a spider's web covered with morning dew were all a cause for gratitude in Siberia. As Andrew says, "It was a chance to celebrate the beauty of life, of nature, a reminder that there was still good in the world."

"If we can live in gratefulness today, the regrets of the past and the worries of the future disappear. By practicing gratefulness, we move out of the self, we slow down and appreciate the present. And the more we practice gratefulness, the more grateful we become."

WHAT YOU CAN DO

☐ Can you think of something you went through that was difficult? Looking back on it, can you find something that you learned or gained from that experience? Could you say that you're thankful for what you may have learned?

☐ Right now, what are three things for which you're thankful?

☐ Is there something you can give to someone less fortunate than you?

☐ Before you even get out of bed in the morning, think of three things for which you're thankful. You could say, "Thank you pillow, thank you blanket, thank you bed." Or "Thank you eyes, thank you ears, thank you lungs." "Thank you sun and light and warmth."

☐ Keep a gratitude journal. Every day, write down three things for which you're thankful.

☐ Write a thank you letter to a teacher or someone who's made a difference in your life.

☐ Say "Thank you" to people around you.

☐ "Stop and smell the roses" is an old saying and a fun practice.

☐ Take time to say a grace before you eat.

DID YOU KNOW? Many scientific studies suggest that people who practice thankfulness are more likely to have higher levels of happiness.

JON KABAT-ZINN (1944–)

U IS FOR UNPLUG

IN THE 1960S, when yoga and meditation were seen as a "far-out hippie thing," Jon Kabat-Zinn brought the lens of science to yoga and meditation.

Jon received his PhD in molecular biology from MIT and conducted research on the effects of meditation on the brain. He found so many measurable benefits that he wanted to share the techniques of yoga and meditation with more people. So, in 1979, he founded the Stress Reduction Clinic. The clinic teaches eight-week courses known as Mindfulness-Based Stress Reduction (MBSR) in which participants routinely experience such beneficial results as reduced pain, a boosted immune system, the ability to sleep better, and an increased ability to cope with stress, anxiety, pain, and illness.

A MBSR student learns to be not a passive patient, but an active participant in their own health and wellness. They commit to setting aside time during the day for peace and quiet. During these moments,

unplug

they are taught to slow down, tune out outer stimuli, and tune into their own breathing, the sensations in the body, and the flowing movement of thoughts in their mind. Without judgment, they pay careful attention to their moment-to-moment experience of living.

Jon calls this "practicing mindfulness," and he doesn't limit mindfulness to meditation. He explains, "We practice mindfulness by remembering to be present in all our waking moments. We can practice taking out the garbage mindfully, eating mindfully, driving mindfully. We can practice navigating through all the ups and downs we encounter, the storms of our minds and the storms of our bodies, the storms of the outer life and of the inner life. We learn to be aware of our fears and our pain, yet at the same time stabilized and empowered by a connection to something deeper within ourselves, a discerning wisdom that helps to penetrate and transcend the fear and the pain, and to discover some peace and hope within our situation as it is."

"You can't stop the waves, but you can learn to surf."

Jon Kabat-Zinn claims that the techniques taught in the Stress Reduction Clinic are age-old practices, nothing new. His clinic now serves as a model for more than seven hundred medical centers and clinics across the country and around the world.

WHAT YOU CAN DO

- ☐ Notice your habits. First thing in the morning, do you reach for your device and check in with the outer world? Or do you check in with your own self, your body and how it feels, the thoughts in your mind, your intentions for the day...?

- ☐ Make a daily habit of taking time to unplug, stretch, breathe, and enjoy quietness.

- ☐ Being sick in bed can be a drag, but it does offer an opportunity to slow down. Instead of immediately plugging into work or entertainment, try plugging into your own body. Ask it what it needs. How can you support it?

- ☐ You can practice mindfulness every day—when you're doing a chore, on your way somewhere, or sitting at your desk.

- ☐ Notice your posture. Can you straighten your back? Notice your breathing. Can you let it flow?

- ☐ Being in nature offers opportunities to unplug. Go on a hike, canoe, camp, or simply enjoy quietness. Practice being in the present moment.

DID YOU KNOW? Did you know that there is a practice called "forest bathing"? If a person simply visits a forest or a group of trees and walks in a relaxed way, they can experience calming, rejuvenating, and restorative benefits.

MARSHALL ROSENBERG (1934–2015)

V IS FOR VOICE

WHEN MARSHALL ROSENBERG was nine years old, his family moved to an inner-city neighborhood in Detroit, Michigan. It was one week before the 1943 Detroit race riots that left thirty-four people dead and six hundred injured.

This early exposure to violence and conflict led Marshall to an interest in resolving conflict peacefully. He pursued a degree in clinical psychology and went on to create a technique known as nonviolent communication, or NVC—a four-step process that helps people clarify and exchange the information necessary to resolve differences peacefully.

NVC avoids using language of blame, judgment, or domination. It teaches us how to listen closely, to our own and to others' feelings. It teaches us to be clear about our own needs, and to express that information in words. It can stretch our understanding of other people,

voice

from enemy to fellow human being. It develops compassion. It creates a path for healing and reconciliation. It can be used on personal, professional, and political levels.

Marshall started using nonviolent communication in the 1960s, mediating between rioting students and college administrators, with civil rights activists, and with people involved in desegregating public schools. Marshall founded a Center for Nonviolent Communication, to train others in the use of this method. He provided NVC training to people in more than sixty countries, including war-torn areas and economically disadvantaged countries.

"Classifying and judging people promotes violence."

Marshall said that nonviolent communication contains nothing new. It is simply based on historic principles of nonviolence—the natural state of compassion, when no violence is present in the heart.

WHAT YOU CAN DO

☐ Here are the four steps in Marshall Rosenberg's problem-solving NVC process. This process helps people understand themselves and others with more clarity and compassion.

1. Observe neutrally, without judging or blaming yourself or the other person.

2. Express your feelings.

3. Clarify and express your needs.

4. Make a specific request.

The process takes a lot of practice, but those are the basics. If you have an issue with someone, you can try these four steps first, as a writing exercise for yourself, or to clarify issues in your own mind.

☐ If someone has hurt your feelings, what can you do?

☐ Is name-calling ever productive? Can it ever help you and the person you're mad at to see eye-to-eye?

☐ When you're filled with anger, is that a good time to communicate? Can you genuinely hear the other person when you're mad? Can you be neutral when you're angry?

DID YOU KNOW? Marshall Rosenberg used two furry puppets as props in his nonviolent communication training—usually a giraffe and a jackal.

RACHEL CARSON (1907–1964)

W IS FOR WONDER

RACHEL CARSON was a scientist, conservationist, and writer with a deep understanding of natural history. She saw humans as part of an intricate web of life. With the onset of the indiscriminate use of chemical pesticides after World War II, Carson observed the destruction of this web of life. In defense of the natural world, Rachel wrote the book *Silent Spring* in 1962. *Silent Spring* is credited with catalyzing the global environmental movement.

In her groundbreaking book, Rachel informed the unsuspecting public about dangerous chemicals that were being sprayed over farms, forests, neighborhoods, and even playgrounds. The chemicals were intended to control pests and disease, but had unintended consequences of contaminating the rivers, groundwater, and soil, and the fish, birds, reptiles, animals, and humans who lived on, in, or near them.

Rachel overlaid these alarming facts with a broader picture: "It took hundreds of millions of years to produce the life that now inhabits

wonder

the earth—eons of time in which that developing and evolving and diversifying life reached a state of adjustment and balance with its surroundings." Rachel challenged the practices of the agricultural scientists and the government, and the worldview from which their practices stemmed. Instead of humans arrogantly controlling nature, she advocated for humility toward "the vast forces" of life.

Rachel wasn't the first or the only person to raise concerns about the hazards of pesticides, but she did gather disparate data into a comprehensive study. She also possessed a unique set of factors that made her a strong spokesperson. Since childhood, Rachel possessed a love of nature and writing. Through working for fifteen years as a scientist and writer for the US Bureau of Fisheries, she was able to combine those two passions and hone the ability to take dense scientific data and break it down into understandable language for everyday people. Through her federal service work, Rachel also made many valuable connections, which helped with collecting data and communicating with people in authority. Additionally, prior to *Silent Spring*, Rachel had already published numerous nature articles and books, including the prize-winning bestseller *The Sea Around Us*. This gave her a measure of fame—both with the scientific community, who lauded her accuracy, and with the public, who appreciated her accessibility. Underlying all these facets, Rachel had a deep love of the natural world and a willingness to be a voice for it.

Rachel Carson's voice reached around the world, into both the public sector and places of authority, sparking environmental awareness and activism. As a result, environmental protections were enacted into law. Though the chemical corporations attacked her, Rachel's voice remained calm and firm and clear.

WHAT YOU CAN DO

☐ Rachel Carson visited the ocean for the first time after college. When she put her feet in the water, fish came to investigate. She was so excited that tears came to her eyes. Is there something joyful that brings tears to your eyes? What makes you feel alive?

☐ Howard Thurman says, "Don't ask what the world needs. Ask what makes you come alive and go do it. Because what the world needs is people who have come alive." Write a list of things that make you come alive. Can you do or follow any of those interests? Is there an *intersection* of your interests and what the world might need?

☐ Rachel Carson found a way to combine her love of writing with her love of nature. Can you combine the things that interest you?

☐ Draw pictures of natural things you are interested in. Describe them in writing.

☐ Join your school's science club or literary club or ask your teachers to help start one.

☐ Celebrate Earth Day on April 22.

DID YOU KNOW?

When *Silent Spring* was published in 1962, it became a *New York Times* bestseller, selling over 500,000 copies in twenty-four countries. It represented a watershed moment of raising public awareness and concern for the environment.

Though she died in 1964, Rachel Carson's legacy played a large role in the founding of Earth Day in 1970.

X = YOUR ACTION

X MARKS THE SPOT where you stand here and now. No need to wait for the future. Today is ripe with opportunities for peaceful activism.

If you want to be an uplifting force in the world, a good way to start is by taking care of yourself. If you take time to take care of your body, mind, and spirit, you'll be better for yourself and everyone around you. Find what gives you energy.

Thich Nhat Hanh says a smile is "the most basic form of peace work." When you smile, it makes you feel good. When you smile at another, it makes them feel good!

All the activists in this book were not born as fully developed activists. They studied, traveled, learned skills, practiced instruments, played sports, experimented, made mistakes, and used their experiences and interests as building blocks. If they had difficult experiences, they transformed those into something useful, or they looked for ways to heal or adapt. Do you have a particular interest? Follow it! A talent? Develop it! A skill? Use it! Did you overcome difficulties? Share it! Are you having a rough time? Reach out for a helping hand! And keep your eye open for places where you can offer your helping hands.

Whether it's what you're doing, or how you're doing it, there's a way to do it mindfully. Whether you're volunteering at a soup kitchen or setting the table at home, whether you're doing what you love or doing what you have to do, whether you've had a choice in your circumstances or not, look for ways to bring love into the picture.

Start small. Start where you are. We all find our way as we go!

X marks the spot

RIGOBERTA MENCHÚ TUM (1959–)

Y IS FOR YEARN

RIGOBERTA MENCHÚ TUM was born in Guatemala and was raised in the tradition of the Mayan indigenous people called the K'iche'. The Mayans developed a rich civilization that dates back thousands of years. Over the past five hundred years, through European expansionism and colonization, the Mayan people have been treated with injustice, intolerance, and violence. The colonial powers didn't even grant citizenship or land rights to the original inhabitants.

The Menchú family were poor peasants. The food they grew in their mountain community was not enough to feed them. When Rigoberta was growing up, she and her family would leave their home for six months out of the year to work under terrible conditions on the coffee and sugar plantations.

Sparked by a US-backed overthrow of the Socialist government, a military regime took over Guatemala in 1960. They ruled the country

yearn

harshly, tolerating little protest or disagreement. Over the course of thirty-six years, the Guatemalan state led a coordinated campaign of violence against the civilian population. Whole villages were wiped out. Two hundred thousand people were killed. Among them were both of Rigoberta's parents, and six other family members.

Due to her personal conviction and sense of justice, Rigoberta became involved with various groups working for basic human rights for the Mayan people. But her organizing efforts caught the attention of the military, and Rigoberta had to flee Guatemala.

During her time abroad, she met many people who were sympathetic to the plight of the Indigenous people. They persuaded her to write a book about her experiences. The result was *I, Rigoberta Menchú*. It was translated into twelve languages and brought international attention to the horrors taking place in Guatemala, which placed pressure on the Guatemalan government to end the violence.

Rigoberta continued to be a world spokesperson for the Mayan people, finding ways to publicize and organize. For her efforts to bring justice to her people, in 1992 Rigoberta was awarded the prestigious Nobel Peace Prize. The worldwide attention of this award was a contributing factor to the 1996 Peace Accords of Guatemala, which ended the thirty-six-year civil war there and gave many rights back to the Mayan people.

Despite the hardships and grief that she has endured, despite the long road to equality and justice, Rigoberta holds a resilient hope for peace in her native Guatemala. She compares the harmonious patterning of colors in the cloths woven by the Mayan women, to the harmonious coexistence of people that is possible in a culturally diverse country where there is mutual respect.

WHAT YOU CAN DO

☐ To *yearn* means to have an intense feeling of longing, typically for something that one has lost or been separated from. For what do you think Rigoberta Menchú yearns? At our core, do you think all people yearn for the same things?

☐ How has Rigoberta Menchú turned her strong feeling into action? What qualities of character does she call on to carry on her work?

☐ Rigoberta Menchú has a vision for a peaceful world built on mutual respect. How can you teach, learn, and practice respect?

☐ Have you ever experienced something that was unfair? Write about it. Try using Marshall Rosenberg's four steps of nonviolent communication on page 99.

☐ Expose yourself to the rich culture and achievements of the Mayan civilization.

☐ The Mayans are expert artisans, creating elaborate, beautiful works in many mediums. Either on your own or in school, make a Mayan mask, mural, or *stela* (an inscribed stone). (See Resources.)

DID YOU KNOW?

Currently there are twenty-one different Mayan languages spoken in Guatemala, but the official language is Spanish. Rigoberta Menchú spoke the language of the K'iche' Indians. In order to be able to communicate more widely, she taught herself Spanish when she was nineteen years old.

Guatemala is touted as the birthplace of chocolate, which Mayans call the "food of the gods."

JULIA CHILD (1912-2004)

Z IS FOR DO IT WITH ZEST

JULIA CHILD came upon her calling relatively late in life: "I was thirty-two when I started cooking; up until then I just ate." Julia was thirty-six when she and her husband moved to France and he introduced her to French cuisine, describing it as "a combination of national sport and high art." Julia called her first meal in Rouen, France, a culinary revelation, "an opening up of the soul and spirit for me."

Now that there was an opening, Julia dove right in. She studied at the Cordon Bleu in Paris, and worked tirelessly to develop reliable, understandable recipes for the American kitchen. *Mastering the Art of French Cooking*, published in 1961, is still in print. The result of much tasting and testing with her two French coauthors, the 726-page cookbook is lauded for making fine cuisine accessible. Julia's advice: "Learn

do it with zest

how to cook—try new recipes, learn from your mistakes, be fearless, and above all, have fun!"

Mastering the Art of French Cooking, considered a seminal culinary work, sealed Julia's reputation and launched her career. *The French Chef*, the first of her many TV series, brought Julia and fine cooking into a bigger spotlight. This was at a time in America when convenience foods were big; TV dinners, canned soups, and frozen vegetables were seen by feminists as enabling women to unchain themselves from the kitchen. Meanwhile, Julia Child was calling people of all genders into the kitchen. Instead of seeing cooking as a menial task, she saw it as an art, a joy, and a deep pleasure. Instead of relying on big companies to process old food from far away, Julia encouraged people to connect with local growers. "You don't have to cook fancy or complicated masterpieces—just good food from fresh ingredients."

"Find something you're passionate about and keep being tremendously interested in it."

Julia helped take food out of the hands of big, multinational corporations and bring it back into the home kitchen to be prepared and enjoyed. She did it all with a cheery enthusiasm, a what-the-hell attitude, and a distinctively charming, bubbly voice!

WHAT YOU CAN DO

☐ If you have special recipes treasured by your family, cook them with your parents and grandparents, aunts and uncles, siblings and cousins. Recognize the recipes and foods that are special to you and part of who you are.

☐ Celebrate your family and cultural traditions. Invite friends to come to dinner and share your traditions with them.

☐ Julia Child's zest for cooking helped to create a cooking revolution. There are now dozens of broadcast and streaming cooking shows, and a whole network dedicated to them. You can learn about cooking by watching them.

☐ Julia Child cooked with zest. Find something that you're passionate about—you may be surprised where that interest will lead you. You can dance with zest, sing with zest, do anything with zest. What calls you?

☐ Create a cookbook of treasured family recipes. Use stories and photos too.

DID YOU KNOW?

Julia Child was six foot two inches tall and played basketball for Smith College.

An exploded duck and an oven fire was the result of one of Julia Child's earliest attempts at cooking.

Mastering the Art of French Cooking took Julia Child nine years to write and get published!

RESOURCES, WEBSITES, AND MORE

Appreciate: Autumn Peltier
Tudor, Aslan and Kelly Tudor. *Young Water Protectors: A Story About Standing Rock.* Seattle, WA: CreateSpace, 2018.

https://www.smithsonianmag.com/blogs /national-museum-american-indian/2018/10/08 /indigenous-peoples-day-2018/

Visual maps of the world's watersheds: https://www.visualcapitalist.com/maps-worlds -watersheds/

The Gifts of the Seven Grandfathers: http:// ojibwe.net/projects/prayers-teachings/the-gifts -of-the-seven-grandfathers/

Waterkeeper Alliance: https://waterkeeper.org

Breathe: Thich Nhat Hanh
Nhat Hanh, Thich. *How to Sit.* Berkeley, CA: Parallax Press, 2014.

Plum Village Community of Engaged Buddhism: https://plumvillage.org

Plum Village app: https://plumvillage.app/

Conserve: John Muir
Muir, John. *John Muir, Selected Writings.* New York, NY: Everyman's Library, 2017.

National Parks Conservation Association: https://www.npca.org

The Sierra Club: https://www.sierraclub.org

The Nature Conservancy: https://www.nature.org/en-us/

Conservation International: https:www.conservation.org

Dream: Martin Luther King Jr.
King Jr, Martin Luther and Kadir Nelson, illus. *I Have a Dream.* New York, NY: Schwartz & Wade, 2012.

The King Center in Atlanta: http://thekingcenter.org

"I Have a Dream" speech: http://www.youtube.com/watch?v=I47Y6VHc3Ms

Empower: Ruth Johnson Colvin
Colvin, Ruth J. *Off the Beaten Path: Stories of People Around the World.* Syracuse, NY: Syracuse University Press, 2012.

ProLiteracy: https://www.proliteracy.org

Room to Read: https://www.roomtoread.org

Feed: Leah Penniman
Book Penniman, Leah. *Farming While Black: Soul Fire Farm's Practical Guide to Liberation on the Land.* White River Junction, VT: Chelsea Green Publishing, 2018.

Soul Fire Farm: http://www.soulfirefarm.org/

National Portrait Gallery, George Washington Carver: https://npg.si.edu/learn/classroom- resource/george-washington-carver-scientist -and-miracle-worker

National Farm to Schools Network: http://www.farmtoschool.org/

Inventions of nineteenth-century black farmers in the United States: https://www.nationalgeographic.org/news /african-american-inventors-19th-century/

Go Local: Alice Waters
Waters, Alice L., and Ann Arnold, illus. *Fanny at Chez Panisse: A Child's Restaurant Adventures with 46 Recipes.* New York, NY: William Morrow Cookbooks, 1997.

Find a local CSA: https://www.localharvest.org/csa

Help build a local economy: https://bealocalist.org

Urban Farms near you:
https://www.urbanfarming.org/garden
-locations.html

American Community Garden Association:
https://communitygarden.org

Help: Ella Baker

Williams, Lea E. *We Who Believe in Freedom: The Life and Times of Ella Baker*. Raleigh, NC: North Carolina Office of Archives, 2017.

Ella Baker Center for Human Rights:
https://ellabakercenter.org/

The Zinn Project, Teaching People's History:
https://www.zinnedproject.org/materials
/baker-ella/

Civil Rights Activity Book:
https://www.tolerance.org

Fundi: The Story of Ella Baker
http://icarusfilms.com

Illuminate: Sister Helen Prejean

Sundem, Garth. *Real Kids, Real Stories, Real Character: Choices That Matter Around the World*. Golden Valley, MN: Free Spirit Publishing, 2016.

Sister Helen's website:
https://www.sisterhelen.org

The Innocence Project:
https://www.innocenceproject.org

Amnesty International: https://www.amnesty.org

Parallax Press: https://www.parallax.org/about

Juxtapose: Valarie Kaur

Applegate, Katherine, and Charles Santoso, illustrator. *Wishtree*. New York, NY: Feiwel and Friends, 2017.

Valarie's TED Talk:
https://www.ted.com/speakers/valarie_kaur

The Revolutionary Love Project:
http://www.revolutionarylove.net/

Understanding Prejudice Activities:
https://secure.understandingprejudice.org
/teach/elemact.htm

Kneel: Colin Kaepernick

Book Macnalie, Joa, and Adua Hernandez, illustrator. *The Hero in the Helmet: Colin Kaepernick*. Lewes, DE: Melanin Origins, 2018.

Colin's website, with lists of the charities he has donated to: https://kaepernick7.com/

Racial Equity Resource Guide (how to find groups near you): https://www
.racialequityresourceguide.org

Amnesty International's Ambassador of Conscience Award: www.amnesty.org/en
/latest/news/2018/04/colin-kaepernick
-ambassador-of-conscience/

Laugh: Norman Cousins

Dahl, Roald. *Roald Dahl Whoppsy-Whiffling Joke Book*. New York, NY: Puffin Books, 2018.

The Laughter Yoga Institute:
https://lyinstitute.org

Laughter Yoga University:
https://laughteryoga.org

World Laughter Day:
https://www.worldlaughterday.com

Make Friends: Azim Khamisa

Book Palacio, R. J. *Wonder*. New York, NY: Knopf Books for Young Readers, 2012.

Tariq Khamisa Foundation: https://tkf.org

Global Art Project for Peace:
https://www.globalartproject.org

Mayo Clinic on forgiveness:
https://www.mayoclinic.org/healthy-lifestyle
/adult-health/in-depth/forgiveness/
art-20047692

Nurture: Shinichi Suzuki

Ryan, Pam Munoz. *Echo*. New York, NY: Scholastic Press, 2015.

The Suzuki Association of the Americas: https://suzukiassociation.org

TedEd Video: How playing an instrument benefits your brain by Anita Collins: http://www.youtube.com/watch?v=R0JKCYZ8hng

Hungry for Music: https://hungryformusic.org

Observe: Jane Goodall

Goodall, Jane. *My Life with the Chimpanzees*. New York, NY: Aladdin, 1996.

The Jane Goodall Institute: https://www.janegoodall.org

Jane Goodall's Roots & Shoots: https://www.rootsandshoots.org

National Audubon Society: https://www.audubon.org

National Geographic: https://www.nationalgeographic.org

Raising Butterflies: https://www.raisingbutterflies.org

Plant: Wangari Maathai

Swanson, Jennifer. *Environmental Activist Wangari Maathai (Stem Trailblazer Biographies)*. Minneapolis, MN: Lerner Publications, 2018.

The Queen of Trees, a movie

Arbor Day Foundation: https://www.arborday.org/

Quest: Black Elk

Books Nelson, S. D. *Black Elk's Vision: A Lakota Story*. New York, NY: Abrams, 2010.

George, Jean Craighead. *My Side of the Mountain*. New York, NY: Dutton Books for Young Readers, 1988.

de Angeli, Marguerite. *The Door in the Wall*. New York, NY: Yearling, 1990.

List of North American powwows: https://www.powwows.com/pow-wows-in-my-state-pow-wow-calendar

Represent: Shirley Chisholm

Book Harrison, Vashti. *Little Leaders: Bold Women in Black History*. Boston, MA: Little, Brown Books for Young Readers, 2017.

Shirley Chisholm Had Guts, a mini documentary by Rachel Maddow: https://www.youtube.com/watch?v=M8uv-uV3XwY

Create your own Women's History Museum: https://www.womenshistory.org/resources/lesson-plan/create-your-own-womens-history-museum

#Lead Like a Girl: https://girl2leader.org (from Woman Political Leaders Global Forum)

Sing: Pete Seeger

MacCarry, Noel. *Who Was Pete Seeger?* New York, NY: Penguin Workshop, 2017.

Hudson River Sloop Clearwater: https://www.clearwater.org

Rise Up and Sing Songbook: https://www.riseupandsing.org

Thank: Andrew Bienkowski

Swamp, Chief Jake, and Erwin Printup Jr., illustrator. *Giving Thanks: A Native American Good Morning Message*. New York, NY: Lee & Low Books, 1997.

Good Days Start with Gratitude: A 52-Week Guide to Cultivate an Attitude of Gratitude: Gratitude Journal. Seattle, WA: Pretty Simple Press, 2017.

Gratefulness: https://gratefulness.org

Nine gratitude activities for kids: http://investinginchildren.on.ca/blog/2015/1/28/9-gratitude-activities-for-children

Unplug: Jon Kabat-Zinn

Nhat Hanh, Thich and Vriezen, Wietske, illustrator. *A Handful of Quiet: Happiness in Four Pebbles.* Berkeley, CA: Plum Blossom, 2007.

Grossman, Laurie. *Master of Mindfulness: How to Be Your Own Superhero in Times of Stress.* Emeryville, CA: Instant Help, 2016.

Meditation for kids:
https://www.headspace.com/meditation/kids

Forest Bathing:
https://www.shinrin-yoku.org/shinrin-yoku.html

Mindful.org: https://www.mindful.org
/meditation/mindfulness-getting-started

Voice: Marshall Rosenberg

Allen, J. P., Marci Winters, and Tamara Laporte, illustrator. *Giraffe Juice: The Magic of Making Life Wonderful.* Honolulu, HI: Giraffe Juice, 2010.

Wolk, Tania, Lind, Brita, and Tamara Laporte, illustrator. *Giraffe Juice Workbook: A Nonviolent Communication Games Book.* Giraffejuice. com, 2010.

Nonviolent Communication:
https:// www.nonviolentcommunication.com

Activities you can ask your teachers to use in your school: http://users.ipfw.edu/lind
/activities.html

Short video about Nonviolent Communication by PowTown: https://www.youtube.com
/watch?v=mS1uDa4tTSM

Wonder: Rachel Carson

Carson, Rachel. *The Sense of Wonder: A Celebration of Nature for Parents and Children.* New York, NY: Harper (1996)

Bruchac, Joseph and Locker, Thomas, illustrator. *Rachel Carson: Preserving a Sense of Wonder.* Golden, CO: Fulcrum Publishing (2004)

The Rachel Carson Homestead:
http://rachelcarsonhomestead.org

Silent Spring Institute:
https://silentspring.org

Rachel Carson Trails Conservancy:
www.rachelcarsontrails.org

Rachel Carson Institute: www.chatham.edu
/centers/rachelcarson

Yearn: Rigoberta Menchú

Menchú, Rigoberta, and Domi, illustrator. *The Girl from Chimel.* Toronto, ON: Groundwood Books, 2005.

Rigoberta Menchú's Nobel Peace Prize lecture: https://www.nobelprize.org/prizes/peace/1992
/tum/lecture

Peace Jam (Nobel Peace Prize winners mentoring youth: https://www.peacejam.org

Three Mayan art projects:
https://www.basd.net/cms/lib2
/PA01001269/Chttp://www.mexicolore
.co.uk/maya/teachers/resource-just-how
-advanced-were-theyentricity/Domain/363
/MayaandAztecArtprojects.pdf

Vani, Supriya. *Battling Injustice: 16 Women Nobel Peace Laureates.* New York: HarperCollins, 2017.

Zest: Julia Child

Edgers, Geoff, and Hempel, Carlene. *Who Was Julia Child?* New York, NY: Penguin Workshop, 2015.

The French Chef: https://www.pbs.org/food
/julia-child/julia-child-video-collection

The Julia Child Foundation:
https://juliachildfoundation.org

How to make a family cookbook:
https://www.greatschools.org/gk/articles
/make-a-family-cookbook

ACKNOWLEDGMENTS

It takes a village to make a book! I'll start by thanking my mother, Marcella Zabinski, who introduced me to many of the peaceful activists included in this book. Thank you to my late father, Roman Zabinski, who surrounded me with art and nurtured the artist in me. Thanks to my husband, Joe DiPasquale, who gives support from every direction. Thank you to my sons, Arlo and Roman DiPasquale, for their honest and perceptive feedback; to Ani DiFranco for all of the love and light she has provided to me; to my sister Nina Gormley for her editorial prowess and conceptual input; to my artist friends Juliet Bice, Katie Reimers, Christy Field, Bret Garwood, Dave Alessi, Sarah Franklin, Diane Schaefer, Amy Vanderwater, Tinya Seeger, Laylah Ali, Georgiana Pickett, Kristin Marfoglia, Melanie Morse, Christine Gallo, and Monique Watts for encouragement and constructive criticism. Thank you to all of my friends and relatives who took an active interest in helping me: Julie and Zachary Smith, Rio and Ron Ross, Dave Zabinski, Jonathan Gormley, Michael Anderson, Jim Pacer, Elisabeth Samuels, Grace Meibohm, Karen Lewis, Tom DiPasquale, Rosanne Pera, Steve Clancy, Brian Lampkin, Michelle Perkins, Leslie Pickering, and Theresa Baker. Thank you to all my teachers. Thank you to all of the peaceful activists in this book for living in creative, pioneering, and inspiring ways. Thank you to the Society of Children's Book Writers and Illustrators for their work, and to Tomie dePaola for reaching out a helping hand. Thank you to Mary Cay Neal and the Buffalo Suzuki Strings community. Thank you to Amber Wigent, Suellen Bielhe, and the people of the Greenville Montessori School in North Carolina for recognizing potential and using the peaceful actions as part of their curriculum! Thank you to Maude White who connected me to my incredibly supportive agent, Joan Brookbank. Thank you to Lori Brown Patrick for helping me hone my writing style. Thank you to everyone at Parallax Press who enabled me to bring this project to life, including my editors Jacob Surpin, Hisae Matsuda, and Teja Watson, art director Terri Saul, and designer Debbie Berne. Thank you to my Planet Love customers who have given me so much encouragement and support. Thank you to Penguin Random House for bringing this to the larger world. Thank you to you, dear reader, and to all the loving energies that circulate around us.

ABOUT THE AUTHOR

TANYA ZABINSKI is a daughter, sister, wife, and mother. She grew up in Buffalo, New York, with nurturing parents and four siblings. Art, music, literature, yoga, gardening, camping, hiking, biking, and spiritual exploration were all a part of her life growing up. In college she studied art, music and philosophy in Buffalo, New York City, and Japan. She and her husband run Planet Love, their own art-based business, exhibiting at more than twenty outdoor art and music festivals per year. Instantly recognizable to those who know and love her art, Tanya's silkscreened images reach a wide audience through printing on the accessible media of T-shirts, banners, and paper. Tanya views life as the ultimate artwork. Her wish is captured in this Sanskrit prayer:

May all beings everywhere be happy and free, and may the thoughts, words, and actions of my own life contribute in some way to that happiness and to that freedom for all.

To find out more about Tanya and her work, go to tanyazabinski.com and peaceloveaction.com.

To Marcella Zabinski, my dynamic mother

✿ PLUM BLOSSOM BOOKS

Plum Blossom Books, the children's imprint of Parallax Press, publishes books on mindfulness for young people and the grown-ups in their lives.

Parallax Press
2236 Sixth Street, Unit B
Berkeley, California 94710
parallax.org

Parallax Press is the publishing division of Plum Village Community of Engaged Buddhism, Inc.

Printed in Canada

Author's note: The people in this book are not saints or gods. They're humans. That means that just like you and me, they're not perfect. They make mistakes. They're learning. Certain aspects of their lives are used here to illustrate peaceful actions. There may be other aspects of their lives that aren't as exemplary. This doesn't invalidate the good they've shared. It just shows that they have room to grow.

The wood pulp used to make this paper is sourced from a sustainable, well-managed forest and is eco-friendly.

Library of Congress Cataloging-in-Publication Data
Names: Zabinski, Tanya, 1963- author.
Title: Peace, love, action!: everyday acts of goodness from A to Z / Tanya Zabinski ; foreword by Ani DiFranco.
Description: Berkeley, California : Plum Blossom Books, [2019] | Audience: Ages: 8 to 12. | Audience: Grades: 7 to 8.
Identifiers: LCCN 2019007011 (print) | LCCN 2019018202 (ebook) | ISBN 9781946764485 (Ebook) | ISBN 9781946764478 (hardcover) | ISBN 9781952692512 (paperback)
Subjects: LCSH: Social reformers—Biography—Juvenile literature. | Social change—History—Juvenile literature. | Social action—Juvenile literature.
Classification: LCC HN8 (ebook) | LCC HN8 .Z33 2019 (print) | DDC 303.4—dc23
LC record available at https://lccn.loc.gov/2019007011

1 2 3 4 5 / 26 25 24 23